# Mark Zuckerberg

ROBIN S. DOAK

**Children's Press®**
An Imprint of Scholastic Inc.

**Content Consultant**
James Marten, PhD
Professor and Chair, History Department
Marquette University
Milwaukee, Wisconsin

Library of Congress Cataloging-in Publication Data
Doak, Robin S. (Robin Santos), 1963–
 Mark Zuckerberg / by Robin S. Doak.
     pages cm. — (A true book)
 Includes bibliographical references and index.
 Audience: Ages 9–12.
 Audience: Grade 4 to 6.
 ISBN 978-0-531-21594-4 (library binding) — ISBN 978-0-531-21756-6 (pbk.)
1. Zuckerberg, Mark, 1984– —Juvenile literature. 2. Facebook (Firm) —Juvenile literature.
3. Facebook (Electronic resource) —Juvenile literature. 4. Online social networks —Juvenile
literature. 5. Webmasters—United States—Biography—Juvenile literature. 6. Businessmen—
United States—Biography—Juvenile literature. I. Title.
 HM479.Z83D627 2015
 006.7092—dc23 [B]                                                 2014048004

© 2016 Scholastic Inc.
All rights reserved. Published in 2016 by Children's Press, an imprint of Scholastic Inc. Published
simultaneously in Canada. Printed in China 62
SCHOLASTIC, CHILDREN'S PRESS, A TRUE BOOK™ and associated logos are trademarks and/or
registered trademarks of Scholastic Inc.
1 2 3 4 5 6 7 8 9 10 R 25 24 23 22 21 20 19 18 17 16

**Front cover: Mark Zuckerberg
speaking at Facebook headquarters
in Menlo Park, California**

**Back cover: Zuckerberg at the TechCrunch
Conference in San Francisco, California**

# Find the Truth!

**Everything** you are about to read is true *except* for one of the sentences on this page.

Which one is **TRUE**?

**T or F**  Mark Zuckerberg became one of the world's richest people before he was 30 years old.

**T or F**  Mark Zuckerberg graduated at the top of his class at Harvard.

Find the answers in this book.

# Contents

## THE BIG TRUTH!

### The Other Facebook Founders

Facebook employs thousands of people around the world.

A 2010 movie about Zuckerberg and Facebook was a smash hit.

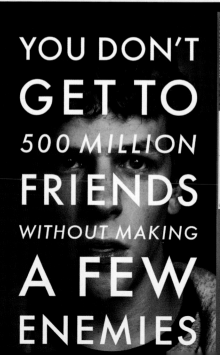
the social network

YOU DON'T GET TO 500 MILLION FRIENDS WITHOUT MAKING A FEW ENEMIES

# CHAPTER 1

# Early Years

In early 2004, no one had heard of a computer Web site called Facebook. Ten years later, the **social networking site** boasted 1.23 billion users around the world. Every day, 757 million members log in and see what their friends and family members are up to.

Mark Zuckerberg is the man behind Facebook. He is known and recognized everywhere. His program, launched from a college dormitory room, has made him one of the richest people in the world.

Zuckerberg's Google+ profile says that he "makes stuff."

# Growing Up

Mark Elliot Zuckerberg was born on May 14, 1984, in White Plains, New York. His father, Ed, was a dentist in the small town of Dobbs Ferry, where the family lived. Mark's mother, Karen, was a **psychiatrist**.

Mark was the second of four children. His older sister, Randi, was born in 1982. Donna was born in 1987. Arielle, the baby of the family, was born in 1989.

As a child, Mark built his own computer games. He used artwork created by his friends in the games.

**Young Mark smiles for the camera.**

**The Zuckerberg family includes, from left to right, Randi, Arielle, Mark, Karen, and Ed.**

The Zuckerberg family was a close and loving one. Mark's parents encouraged all of their children to do what they loved best. The family valued education and insisted that their kids take school seriously.

Ed Zuckerberg was fascinated by new technology. Years before his kids were born, he had bought one of the earliest personal computers (PCs) for his dental office. The computer was expensive and could not do as much as today's computers.

**The availability and popularity of home computers grew rapidly during the 1990s.**

Growing up, Ed's children each had their own computers. Ed's love of technology rubbed off on Mark. Mark spent hours playing computer games and figuring out how computers worked. In middle school, he began to write computer programs.

One of Mark's first programs was nicknamed "Zucknet." Zucknet allowed the Zuckerbergs to send instant messages to each other from computers in their bedrooms. Ed also used Zucknet in his office.

# A Good Education

Mark's parents encouraged his interest in technology. When Mark was in high school, they hired someone to tutor him in computer science once a week. Mark also began to take graduate-level computer courses at a nearby university.

When Mark was a junior in high school, his parents enrolled him at Phillips Exeter Academy. This high-ranking high school prepares students to enter good colleges. Mark moved to Exeter, New Hampshire, to live at the **boarding school**.

AOL and Microsoft both offered Mark a job when he was still in high school.

**Many of Phillips Exeter's students, including Mark, lived at the school.**

11

Although far from home, Mark did well at the academy. He excelled in science and math. He also loved literature, especially the classics. He took Latin, Greek, and French courses.

Mark made new friends easily. He enjoyed fencing, a sword-fighting sport, and was captain of the school team. He also continued to amaze his friends with his computer programs. In New Hampshire, he founded his first company, Intelligent **Media** Group.

**Mark (left) poses with his teammates on the fencing team.**

# Synapse

In high school, Mark created a music player that he called Synapse. Synapse worked by having users rate songs they heard. Then the program used **artificial intelligence** to choose new songs that the listener might enjoy. Both Microsoft and AOL offered to buy the program, but Mark refused. Instead, he allowed people to use the program for free on the Internet.

# CHAPTER 2

# Facebook Is Born

Zuckerberg graduated from Phillips Exeter in 2002. That fall, the teenager entered Harvard University in Cambridge, Massachusetts.

Just two years into his studies, Zuckerberg created a new computer program. That program would change his future—and revolutionize how people used the Internet.

 Harvard is the oldest university in the United States.

# College Programming

Harvard was a good environment for the young computer **programmer**. Zuckerberg studied computer science and psychology. He quickly became known as a computer whiz. He joined a fraternity and made many good friends.

In his second year of college, Zuckerberg wrote a program called CourseMatch. The program helped students choose which classes to take. It also matched students with each other for study groups.

Another program Zuckerberg created was based on Harvard's "facebooks." These books featured pictures of students who lived in Harvard's dorms. The facebooks helped people living in each dorm get to know one another.

Zuckerberg's version was an online program called Facemash. The site posted photos from the facebooks pages, two at a time. Other students then voted on which student was more attractive.

**Facemash was extremely popular with many Harvard students.**

Zuckerberg's Facemash was popular with many Harvard students. However, many others complained that the site invaded their privacy and used photos without permission. School officials shut the site down. But the site had given Zuckerberg an idea. Why not connect all Harvard students through an online social network?

Zuckerberg and four of his friends began working together to make the idea a reality. The young men worked in Zuckerberg's dorm room.

**Zuckerberg (right) poses with his friend and roommate Dustin Moskovitz on the steps of a Harvard building.**

Why was TheFacebook designed in blue? Zuckerberg is color-blind. He has trouble seeing reds and greens.

In February 2004, Zuckerberg launched TheFacebook.com. At first, the Web site was open only to Harvard students. The idea was for students to upload their photos and type text into a format that Zuckerberg designed. They could also upload other media and create online profiles.

TheFacebook was a success. Within two weeks, half of all students at Harvard had signed up. Over the next few years, TheFacebook spread to other universities and then to high schools.

# The Other Facebook Founders

Five people are credited with creating Facebook. We know Mark Zuckerberg. Here's a look at the other four.

**Chris Hughes**
Hughes lived in the same college dorm as Zuckerberg. He was Facebook's first spokesman, and he created Barack Obama's first Facebook fan page. Today, he is the editor in chief of New Republic magazine.

### Dustin Moskovitz

Moskovitz was Zuckerberg's roommate at Harvard. As the company's first chief technology officer, he was in charge of solving any technological issues. Today, he has his own company, called Asana.

### Andrew McCollum

McCollum (not pictured) is a former Harvard student. A graphic designer, he helped create Facebook's look.

### Eduardo Saverin

Born in Brazil in 1982, Saverin was a junior at Harvard when he met Zuckerberg. He was involved in the earliest phases of developing TheFacebook and was later put in charge of Facebook's finances. He now lives in Singapore.

# CHAPTER 3

# Facebook Moves to California

TheFacebook was different from other social network sites. Other sites were set up to help users meet new people. But TheFacebook was a place to keep in touch with people the users already knew, their own friends and family. Anyone who wanted to sign up for TheFacebook had to register with his or her real name and e-mail address.

By the end of 2004, TheFacebook had more than one million users.

**Palo Alto is the home of many technology companies.**

## A Growing Business

In July 2004, Zuckerberg officially made TheFacebook a **corporation**. He was the company's chief executive officer, or CEO. The company's mission: "To give people the power to share and make the world more open and connected."

Zuckerberg dropped out of Harvard and moved across the country to the West Coast. Some of his friends went with him. The men rented a house in Palo Alto, California.

Zuckerberg's first job was to convince wealthy investors to lend the company money. Luckily, some investors saw the company's potential. They gave hundreds of thousands of dollars to help get TheFacebook off the ground.

The Web site has always been free to users. So how did investors make their money back? The company generates money when advertisers pay to place their ads on the site. As more and more people signed up, advertisers became easier to find.

Only 10 years after becoming a corporation, Facebook earned nearly $12.5 billion a year.

Create social ads

**Facebook Ads**

Create an adver

Promote your business virally to Facebook's 500M+ active users. Click here to crea

25

In 2005, the company dropped "the" from its name and Web site address. The company became, simply, Facebook. As Facebook prospered, other media groups started knocking on Zuckerberg's door. Many of them wanted to buy the new company. In 2006, the Internet company Yahoo offered to pay $1 billion for Facebook. Zuckerberg declined this offer as well as others from Google, Viacom, and MySpace.

# Timeline of Facebook

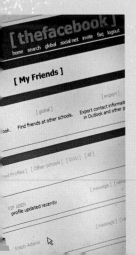

**February 2004**

Zuckerberg and four of his friends create TheFacebook.

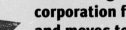

**Summer 2004**

Zuckerberg forms a corporation for TheFacebook and moves to California.

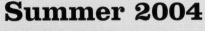

As the Web site grew in popularity, the company grew in size. Over the years, the staff has grown from a few students in a dorm room to nearly 10,000 people.

In 2008, Facebook opened its international headquarters in Dublin, Ireland. Since then, other Facebook offices have opened around the world.

## 2005
Zuckerberg drops "the" from the name and Web site, renaming it "Facebook."

## February 2014
Facebook celebrates its 10th birthday.

## September 2006
Facebook is opened to anyone over 13 years old with an e-mail address. Registration on the site jumps to 50,000 new users each day.

# CHAPTER 4

# The Facebook Community

By his mid-20s, Mark Zuckerberg was one of the richest people in the world. Yet the young **entrepreneur** remains actively involved in the company he founded. On workdays, he dons his familiar hoodie and gray T-shirt and heads into the office. Zuckerberg still serves as the company's CEO. He works to make Facebook a great product and the company a great place to work.

Zuckerberg's friends and employees call him Zuck.

# Working for Zuck

In 2011, Zuckerberg moved his company from Palo Alto to Menlo Park, California. He wanted to attract top-quality programmers and **engineers** to keep Facebook fresh. In the new headquarters, Zuckerberg set about creating a space where workers would want to come every day.

**Facebook headquarters in Menlo Park is a big campus that includes several buildings.**

**Facebook's office space is bright and open.**

# An Open Environment

Inside the building, engineers, programmers, and product testers work at computers on top of desks and tables. There are no cubicles to separate people from one another.

Zuckerberg is a constant presence in the building. He works at the same type of desk as his employees. Co-workers can come to him with questions and concerns, and they say that he is willing to listen. Once a week, he holds a question-and-answer meeting with his employees.

**Facebook headquarters has a number of kitchen areas.**

## Office Life

Other benefits make Facebook a cool place to work. The company offers free meals and snacks to workers. There is even a sit-down restaurant and a sweet shop. There's an on-site gym so workers can exercise, and the company pays for employee health benefits.

Facebook strives to keep its workers creative. Couches and gathering spaces are placed all around the building so people can get together, brainstorm, and talk.

Like Zuckerberg, most of the people who work for the company are young. Their office space reflects that. Bright artwork and basketball courts keep things fun. Of course, there are also gaming stations! Facebook has popped up on lists of the best places to work in the United States. Zuckerberg himself gets high marks as a well-liked and respected leader.

Facebook's "Like" button was almost called the "Awesome" button.

**This chalkboard wall includes notes and doodles from countless Facebook employees.**

One out of every six people in the world is on Facebook.

# CHAPTER 5

# Making a Difference

In 2010, six years after Facebook's founding, Zuckerberg was named *Time* magazine's Person of the Year. The honor acknowledged how much Facebook has changed the way people communicate and share information.

Not all people are Facebook fans. Some people complain that constant and immediate access to thoughts, opinions, and images have had a negative effect on society. Others say the company has too much access to users' online activities both on and off Facebook.

# Sharing the Wealth

Since becoming wealthy, Zuckerberg has given millions of dollars to charity. Both he and his wife, Priscilla Chan, are especially interested in education. One of his earliest large donations was to the school system in Newark, New Jersey.

Another one of Zuckerberg's favorite causes is the Silicon Valley Community Foundation. This group supports smaller local charities. It also offers financial aid to area kids to continue their education.

**Zuckerberg takes part in an assembly at a school to which he donated several laptops.**

# Priscilla Chan

During his sophomore year at Harvard, Zuckerberg met fellow student Priscilla Chan at a party. Chan had been born in Boston, Massachusetts, in 1985. She studied biology at Harvard. She stayed in college after Zuckerberg moved to California and graduated in 2007.

The two dated for nine years before marrying in 2012. Today, Chan is a medical doctor. She and Zuckerberg have a fluffy white dog named Beast. Beast even has his own Facebook page.

**Barack Obama's Facebook activities helped him reach young voters who regularly use the site.**

# Facebook and Politics

Facebook has even influenced U.S. politics. In 2008, Barack Obama was a little-known senator from Illinois running for president. Obama used the social network to spread his message and gain votes. He had earned more than two million followers on Facebook by election time. Other politicians quickly followed Obama's example. They created Facebook pages and used other social media to spread their message. The method was so powerful it became known as the "Facebook effect."

# News on Facebook

Facebook has changed the way news is reported and spread throughout the world. People can now share information, opinions, and news in real time on the Web site. Those who witness or are involved in a story can let others know almost instantly what is happening. In nations where the government controls the news, this instant access has caused problems. China, Egypt, and other countries have banned Facebook during riots and protests.

**Riots, such as the ones in China's Xinjiang region in 2009, have prompted some countries to prevent people from accessing Facebook and spreading news about the events.**

# Fame and Fortune

It's not "all work and no play" for Zuckerberg. His job allows him to travel and meet new and important people. He has met with heads of state, famous inventors, wealthy businesspeople, and superstars.

Zuckerberg has a sense of humor. When *The Simpsons* turned him into a cartoon character, Zuckerberg supplied the voice. He even appeared on *Saturday Night Live*.

**Zuckerberg met with leaders from around the world to discuss Internet security in 2011.**

Jesse Eisenberg was nominated for an Academy Award when he played Zuckerberg in *The Social Network*.

Zuckerberg's success has sometimes made him a target. In 2010, a movie about the history of Facebook was released in theaters. It portrayed the Web site's creation and some of the legal challenges Zuckerberg and the company have faced. *The Social Network* starred many well-known actors and earned awards. The movie showed Zuckerberg in a somewhat negative light. But he has said that he is not like the movie character.

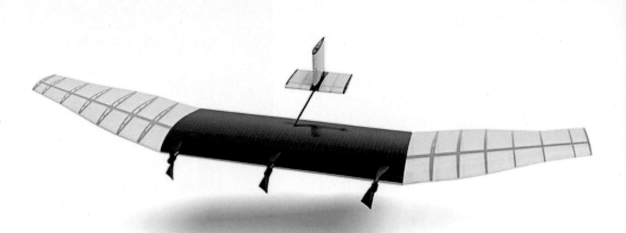

**Drones such as this one could one day bring Internet access to remote places around the world.**

## A New Goal

Zuckerberg continues to look for ways to expand his business and connect people. One of his dreams is to spread low-cost Internet access throughout the world. To this end, he has founded a project called Internet.org. Working with other technology companies, Zuckerberg hopes to build solar-powered **drones**. These would beam the Internet to even the most remote locations.

Zuckerberg dreams of a world where farmers around the globe have instant access to crop and weather reports. He imagines everyone being able to log on to get information about health and medicine. Education could flourish throughout the world.

In February 2014, Facebook celebrated its 10th anniversary. Only time will tell what the next 10 years hold for the company and its founder. But no one can deny that Zuckerberg, a young computer genius, has already left a lasting mark on society. ★

**In 2013, an artist organized an art show in Singapore that included several different portraits of Zuckerberg. The show demonstrated how famous Zuckerberg—and Facebook—have become.**

**Date Zuckerberg was born:** May 14, 1984

**Place Zuckerberg was born:** White Plains, New York

**Zuckerberg's current residence:** Palo Alto, California

**Names of Zuckerberg's parents:** Ed Zuckerberg and Karen Kempner Zuckerberg

**Names of Zuckerberg's sisters:** Randi, Donna, Arielle

**Name of Zuckerberg's wife:** Priscilla Chan (1985–)

**Schools Zuckerberg attended:** Phillips Exeter Academy (2000–2002); Harvard University (2002–2004)

**Zuckerberg's net worth:** More than $30 billion

## Did you find the truth?

Mark Zuckerberg became one of the world's richest people before he was 30 years old.

Mark Zuckerberg graduated at the top of his class at Harvard.

# Resources

## Books

Dobinick, Susan. *Mark Zuckerberg and Facebook*. New York: Rosen, 2013.

Marsico, Katie. *Tremendous Technology Inventions*. Minneapolis: Lerner, 2014.

McClafferty, Carla Killough. *Tech Titans*. New York: Scholastic, 2012.

Yomtov, Nel. *Internet Inventors*. New York: Children's Press, 2013.

# Important Words

**artificial intelligence** (ahr-tuh-FISH-uhl in-TE-luh-juhns) — the science of making computers do things that previously needed human intelligence

**boarding school** (BOR-ding SKOOL) — a school that students may live in during the school year

**corporation** (kor-puh-RAY-shuhn) — a group of people who are allowed by law to run a company as a single person

**drones** (DROHNZ) — remotely controlled aircraft without pilots

**engineers** (en-juh-NEERZ) — people who are specially trained to design and build machines, large structures, or computer systems

**entrepreneur** (ahn-truh-pruh-NUR) — someone who starts businesses and finds new ways to make money

**media** (MEE-dee-uh) — methods of communicating or the materials used to do so

**programmer** (PROH-gram-ur) — a person who writes the instructions to make a computer perform various functions

**psychiatrist** (sye-KYE-uh-trist) — a medical doctor who is trained to treat emotional and mental illness

**social networking site** (SOH-shul NET-wur-king SITE) — a Web site that helps people connect with each other in a friendly way

# Index

Page numbers in **bold** indicate illustrations.

# About the Author

Robin S. Doak has been writing for children for nearly 25 years. A graduate of the University of Connecticut, she loves writing about history makers from the past and the present. Doak lives in Maine with her husband. She uses Facebook to keep track of what her grown kids are up to.